T0198788

DON'T BE AFRAID OF THE DARK™

NICKY MOONBEAM SAVES CHRISTMAS

Author ~ Creator
Wanda Cavaliere

Illustrator ~ Donna Orth

Order this book online at www.trafford.com
or email orders@trafford.com

Most Trafford titles are also available at major online book retailers.

 www.trafford.com

North America & international
toll-free: 844 688 6899 (USA & Canada)
fax: 812 355 4082

Our mission is to efficiently provide the world's finest, most comprehensive book publishing service, enabling every author to experience success. To find out how to publish your book, your way, and have it available worldwide, visit us online at www.trafford.com

Because of the dynamic nature of the Internet, any web addresses or links contained in this book may have changed since publication and may no longer be valid. The views expressed in this work are solely those of the author and do not necessarily reflect the views of the publisher, and the publisher hereby disclaims any responsibility for them.

Any people depicted in stock imagery provided by Getty Images are models,
and such images are being used for illustrative purposes only.
Certain stock imagery © Getty Images.

Artwork, characters, and trademarks are exclusively owned by author.

Illustrated by Donna Orth

ISBN: 978-1-4669-0656-3 (sc)
ISBN: 978-1-4669-7701-3 (e)

Library of Congress Control Number: 2011962028

Print information available on the last page.

Trafford rev. 02/26/2021

To my father, Edward Clifford Askins

Who inspired me to create a children's character, and who at one time told me as a child that God hung the moon as the "Night Light in the Sky" for all the little "children of the world" who whispered to them, "Don't be afraid of the dark!"

To my Mother, Carrie Askins

Thank you for all your encouragement and co-authoring the ABC Book. Thanks for all the test-marketing of the Nicky stories with your Smiley Faces Pre- School students. Dad and you have been such wonderful parents and are a blessing.

To my husband, Chris

Thank you for being my best friend, life partner, and supporter who encouraged me to bring Nicky Moonbeam to the "children of the world" and made it possible. You have added so much depth and joy to my life!

To our son, Michael

Thank you as a child of seven for creating and drawing the Dream Stealer clouds as the protagonists. You are so amazing and excel at everything you undertake.

To my twin, Rev. Fonda Blair

For your dedicated inspirational work as a pastor for twenty years and as a dedicated school teacher for forty years. Having you as a sister, role model, and best girlfriend through life has been a wonderful life experience. Thank you for your creativity and involvement in the early creation of the Nicky character and for the wonderful adventures we took nightly with Nicky Moonbeam as children growing up in Fayetteville, Tennessee.

This one is for you!
Wanda Askins Cavaliere

Created for the "children of the world"

GLOW: Go Light Our World with your special gifts!

One Christmas Eve, after Nicky Moonbeam hugged all the children on Earth good night, he decorated his Christmas tree. Each year Nicky chose the brightest stars in the sky for his tree. The stars that were chosen to adorn Nicky's tree twinkled and glowed with pride. You see, Nicky Moonbeam is The Man in the Moon, and to be chosen as a star to decorate his Christmas tree is a great honor.

The Big Dipper poured Nicky Moonbeam a cup of cocoa. The Little Dipper served Nicky cookies. *What a busy night this has been!* Nicky thought.

Nicky Moonbeam had two important jobs each night. The first was hugging the children before they drifted into dreamland. He loved to stretch his long, moonbeam arms around the Earth to give each child a hug. Nicky's second job was being the Big Night-Light in the sky so children wouldn't be afraid of the dark.

Nicky knew tonight was the night Santa Claus delivered presents to every child. Nicky's good friend, Hailey loved Christmas more than any other holiday. He had met Hailey last summer when she and her family were camping. How Nicky and Hailey laughed when they were together! And what adventures they always had!

Nicky decided to take his sailboat, The Dream Weaver, to his good friend's house so he could wish Hailey a Merry Christmas.

"Hailey, are you asleep?" Nicky asked, as he shined his moonbeams on Hailey's window.

"Tonight is Christmas Eve, Nicky Moonbeam! I can't sleep, I'm too excited!" called Hailey, opening her window to talk to Nicky. "I can hardly wait to see what Santa brings me." Just then, they heard the TOOT!

TOOT! TOOT! of a loud horn.

"What's that noise?" Hailey asked Nicky Moonbeam.

"Oh, my craters! Oh, my moonbeams!" Nicky cried. "Santa must need help! Santa's Chief Elf, Michael, always blows that horn when Santa has an emergency at the North Pole. Hop aboard the Dream Weaver, Hailey. My sailboat will take us to help Santa and his elves."

Nicky and Hailey loved to sail on The Dream Weaver because it took them wherever their imaginations wanted to go. Off they sailed through the glistening snowflakes, floating across the dark sky to the North Pole. The Big Dipper and Little Dipper twinkled on both sides of the sailboat.

Nicky and Hailey could see the North Pole as The Dream Weaver neared Santa's home. Elves scurried everywhere; wrapping the presents Santa would deliver tonight.

The Dream Weaver gently landed at the Candy Cane Parking Lot, in a spot reserved just for The Man in the Moon. Nicky tooted his star horn to announce his arrival. Santa, Mrs. Claus, the reindeer, and the elves ran to greet Nicky and Hailey.

"What's the problem, Santa?" called Nicky.

"I have two problems. Look at the sky, Nicky Moonbeam," replied Santa. "The snow is getting thicker and thicker! Rudolph is sick with a cold and his nose won't glow. Poor Rudolph! The poor children! How can I deliver these gifts if Rudolph can't guide my sleigh? The children will be so disappointed on Christmas morning if there are no gifts under the Christmas tree," Santa groaned.

"Also, I have a second problem. Those four Dream Stealers, Bullee, Whinee, Blamee, and Wimpy are up to their pranks again!" said Santa. "The Elves have reported that the four of them are blowing snow all over the children's beautifully wrapped packages and pelting my reindeer and elves with snowballs. The Elves and Reindeer are taking cover behind the sled," he said. "The Dream Stealers' pranks are slowing me down. My sleigh needs to lift off in an hour or children will wake up on the other side of the world with no toys!" Santa said sadly.

Just at that moment, Bullee, one of the Dream Stealers, floated over to Santa and grabbed his hat. Nicky's moonbeams quickly took the hat back, placing it on his head.

"That Santa hat looks really silly on your head, Nicky," said Bullee.

"That's right, Bullee," said Nicky, "the only person that deserves to wear this hat is Santa Claus!" Nicky handed Santa's hat back to Santa.

Frustrated in losing Santa's hat, Bullee began weaving in and out of the crowd yelling gleefully, "ha ha ha, hee hee hee." Quickly he flew over to Santa's toy sack and grabbed a toy train. Nicky's moonbeams were fast acting, wrapping around Bullee's pincher claws. Nicky handed the train to Ms. Claus.

"Ms. Claus looks ridiculous holding a little boy's train," said Bullee. "That's right Bullee", said Nicky, "this train will be placed back into Santa's sack for a little boy in Tennessee who has it on his Christmas list."

Angrily, Bullee zooms over to his pals, Whinee, Blamee, and Wimpy complaining that he can't have any fun.

"I have a plan," Bullee whispers to his pals. Angrily, he flew high…..then low. He whizzed by Hailey and Chief Elf Michael, glaring his angry red eyes. He quickly reached down…. down….down….. grabbing a doll out of a gift box that one of the Elves was wrapping.

Nicky's magical moonbeams zoomed so fast taking the doll from Bullee and returning the doll to the elf.

"Nicky you ruin all the fun." shouted Bullee.

"This nonsense must stop as Santa's sleigh needs to leave immediately!" said Nicky.

"You are right, Nicky," Santa exclaimed. "We can't let Dream Stealers and mischief get in the way of getting the toys to the children of the world tonight."

The Dream Stealers formed into dark clouds and floated into the night sky. "Nicky Moonbeam you haven't seen the last of us yet," they all shouted together, their angry red eyes glowing against the darkness. They flashed a bolt of lightning and a roar of thunder and disappeared into the blackness.

Suddenly, they hear a very loud sound. Poor Rudolph was sneezing. His nose was stuffed up from Reindeer flu. His throat was sore from coughing. Rudolph's nose did not glow the bright red it usually did. And his eyes were watery, too.

"Rudolph is the only reindeer with a magical red nose," Santa said. I depend on him to light the night sky and guide my sleigh every Christmas Eve. Without Rudolph's glowing light, my sleigh might crash into a house and hurt my reindeer. And if the presents tumble from my bag, the children's toys will be lost. What will we do? " Santa asked.

"Oh, Santa! The children will be so disappointed if gifts aren't under their trees on Christmas morning," Hailey said, her eyes filling with tears. "What can we do to help you Santa?" she asked.

Nicky Moonbeam, wanting to comfort Hailey put one of his long moonbeam arms around her.

"Let's think of a plan," Chief Elf Michael said. Chief Elf Michael was in charge of all emergencies at the North Pole. He blew his emergency horn, wiggled his toes and touched the tip of his nose. That always helped him think of a plan. " I know, Nicky can guide Santa's sleigh tonight with the light of his moonbeams!" he happily chirped.

"Yes! Yes!" cheered Santa and the others. Even Rudolph looked a little happier. "What a fine idea," Santa said. "If your beams guide me, Nicky, I can land on course! My reindeer and all the presents will be safe!"

"Oh, my moonbeams! If I go into my 'new moon' phase, my beams won't glow bright enough to guide the sleigh!" said Nicky.

"You can do it, Nicky Moonbeam!" said Hailey. "All of us will team up to help you!" Hailey whispered in Nicky Moonbeam's ear. "Remember you told me if I believe in myself, I could do anything?" The Man in the Moon nodded yes. "You said each child has a special gift to share with the world and that each child is to **GLOW**: to **G**o **L**ight **O**ur **W**orld with their special gifts. You have a special gift, too, Nicky. Tonight, your gift of light can help save Christmas for children all around the world! So go, and GLOW…Nicky, GO LIGHT OUR WORLD!"

Nicky Moonbeam thought for a moment. "If we all work together, we can save Christmas. What a wonderful gift to give the children. C'mon, let's go!" called Nicky.

"Hooray! We'll help by getting the sleigh loaded quickly!" the Elves shouted.

"I can help Rudolph prepare for the long cold night by putting an ice pack on his head to help his fever, a blanket to keep him warm, and prior to lift-off, feed him warm alphabet soup," said Hailey.

"Even if my nose won't light up, I can still help by reading the map for Santa so we won't miss any of the children's houses!" Rudolph exclaimed as he sneezed.

"And we'll help by guiding you with our brightest light!" called out the stars.

"And we will help the Elves load the rest of the toys," the Dream Stealers shouted.

The Elves and Dream Stealers worked fast loading the last bag of toys on the sleigh. Santa wrapped Rudolph in a thick blanket and Hailey tied a warm muffler around Rudolph's neck.

Nicky Moonbeam waved good-bye to the happy crowd. He returned to the sky as a big, bright, full moon. The stars polished their points, each trying to outshine the others.

Santa's sleigh flew off into the night with Nicky high overhead, dazzling the sleigh with moonbeams, lighting the night sky.

Nicky watched the sleigh take off and land as Santa delivered toys to children around the world.

The light began to fade. Santa had one more house to visit on 210 Mulberry Avenue before every present was delivered.

Nicky's beams began to flicker and dim in the dense fog and snow. "Oh, my moonbeams, I'm fading!" Nicky Moonbeam called. "Hurry, Santa, hurry, if I go into my new moon phase, it will be so dark I cannot guide the sleigh!" said Nicky.

Santa, Hailey, Chief Elf Michael, Rudolph, and the stars chimed in together, "You can do it, Nicky Moonbeam!"

Hailey slid from the sleigh, riding a tiny moonbeam that Nicky had given her to use in an emergency. Then she floated up to Nicky and stretched her tiny arms as far as she could around him. Hailey gave Nicky a GREAT, BIG HUG.

Nicky Moonbeam was so happy; he shined his beams brighter than ever.

Once again, the sky was filled with light, so Santa could land his sleigh at the last house.

As the sleigh returned to the North Pole, the sun began to rise. Nicky, Hailey, Mrs. Claus, Dream Stealers and the Elves clapped as Santa's sleigh landed safely.

"You saved Christmas, Nicky Moonbeam!" said Santa. "Thank you for helping us!" Everyone cheered, "NICKY! NICKY! NICKY!"

Mrs. Claus served hot chocolate and Christmas cookies for the tired crew and the Elves played their favorite Christmas music. Dancer danced with Dasher. Prancer pranced with Comet. Cupid, Vixen, Donner, and Blitzen clapped their hooves. Even Rudolph, who felt much better now that his nose was lighting up, danced with Chief Elf Michael. Santa and Mrs. Claus waltzed together. The Dream Stealers who had returned and were behaving were happy, too. To their delight, Santa left each of them a brand new one hundred mold set because everyone knew that clouds loved to change shapes and confuse everybody. The Elves laughed at all the shapes that Bullee, Whinee, Blamee, and Wimpy were changing into, trying to guess what shapes they were. Bullee, as usual was trying to tell everyone that he was changing into the best shape of all. Hailey and Nicky Moonbeam talked and laughed. The stars skated across the sky.

"I'm so proud of you," Hailey told Nicky Moonbeam. "You saved Christmas," she whispered, falling asleep on Nicky's crescent moon.

"We all saved Christmas, Hailey," Nicky gratefully replied.

Nicky Moonbeam felt happy and loved by all the children on Earth.

Nicky beamed Hailey down to her little bed, cradling her softly on a moonbeam. The moment they arrived, Nicky heard Hailey's parents calling, "Hailey, wake up! Let's go see what Santa has left under the tree!"

Santa barely had enough time to magically whirl up the chimney before Hailey bounded down the steps.

Nicky Moonbeam returned to the sky. He stretched his long moonbeam arms around the Earth to give the children one last hug as they crossed into dream land. Nicky Moonbeam's heart swelled with happiness. He felt loved by and important to every child in the world. Giving to those you love is the best gift of all, he thought to himself. If only you believe, you can achieve anything. Anything can happen if everyone works together, Nicky thought, smiling to himself.

"Merry Christmas, children," Nicky whispered in each child's ear, as he donned his Santa hat and placed a candy cane in the snow.

"Every night, I shine my moonbeams down on you and all the sleeping children. I watch over you as you sleep. Throughout the day you have the sunlight shining on you. During the night, you have my moonbeams and star beams shining into your room, GLOWING all around you, just in case you awake and need my light. And remember, when you are alone in the dark, you have no reason to be afraid. I am your Night Light in the Sky, shining outside your window," said Nicky.

With this, Nicky blew a moonbeam kiss....

....covered in moon dust love to all children....

....where each child travels....to that safe and restful place in their dreams...where each

Child can d-r-e-a-m.... AND be whatever they want to be!

Love,

Your friend,

Nicky Moonbeam, the Man in the Moon, the Night -Light in the Sky

Acknowledgment

Nicky Moonbeam Saves Christmas is the first book in a series of twelve books, titled: "Don't Be Afraid of the Dark." A childhood dream of mine has been fulfilled with the publication of this book and the twelve books to follow. Nicky Moonbeam is for children everywhere.

A thank you to the following people below as you all have been important, either in your support, encouragement, or belief in the Nicky project over the years to benefit the "children of the world."

Larry Askins

Michael Petrone, III, Gage & Gunner

Robert Sherman

Donna Orth, Illustrator

Michelle Canar, Tom Norris

Laurie Curran, former Director Licensing, Hasbro Toys

Bob & Connie Meng

Chuck & Michelle Ecker

Lori Newberg, Brian O'Neil

Immelda & Greg Cleaver

Carolyn Fierro, Editor, Ed Wellmeyer

Lisa Millman Lange, Mike Finamore

Nasrullah, Niazi, Sanam, Soubhan, Ghazl, Joseph

Kent Goss, Esq., John Walton, Esq.

Cindi & Pete Mowery, Rafael Avila

Nick Thomas, Charlotte Bennardo, Author

Carrie Brown

Gigi Askins, Don Theeuwes

Daria Lavelle, Maura & Connor

Dr. Ron Ashton & Louise

Marcia Baker- Editor, Tom Cervanka

Birdie & Don Rice - Rice Prep School

Abe Kleinman, NBTY, (In Memory)

Mike Oliveri, Michelle Classi, Mike Chansilp

Misty Rhodes & Adam, Tom Kroll (In Memory)

Jerry Luttrell, Janice Maer

Ronnie & Jessica Parker & parents

Denny, Steve Chaya & Jay (In Memory)

Ann Powell, Fred I Womack, (In memory)

Nephews' & Nieces: Alex, Austin, Caiden, Alessandra, Kristopher, Brianna

Al Hammack, Esq., David Affeld, Esq.

Sindee Smilowitz, Esq., Rhonda Klick, Esq.

Bonnie Baldridge, Gene Miller

John Ecternach, Theresa Morgan

Lois Stump, (In memory) & Gammy

Jim Loveder, Esq.

Harvey Pasternak, Marci (In Memory) & Girls

Doug Roper, Ted & Connie Tran

Lynn Branch, Matt Griges

Bob Singer, illustrator, Hanna Barbera

American Diabetes Association for publishing Nicky & characters on ADA website for several years

Karen & Bob Brown (In memory)

My former students: Pocatello, Idaho; Elora, Tennessee; Mogadore, Ohio; Flintville, Tennessee; Laredo, Texas; Chadron, Nebraska; Lynchburg, Tennessee; Erin, Tennessee & the 28 children who named Nicky!

Virginia Gonzalez, Carlos, Hannah Su

Lisa & Jim Treadwell, Neil Shah, Alim Javed

Emilio Romeo Buster, Linda Carrier, Tammi Cencke, Pat Cary PBS- Larry Rifkin, Lisa DiDonato Cambria

Kathy, Nissa, Chris, Alan, Elliot, Ken Blake

Sue Lampley, Susan Marx, Sergio Andreoli

Trafford: Edwin Ingram, Evan Villadores, Nick Arden, Jacky Valle, Marie Penares & the Production team

My sincere apology if I have left anyone's name off, as the list is endless!

Wanda Askins Cavaliere, Creator of Nicky Moonbeam

Wanda Cavaliere, Creator of Nicky Moonbeam is a former elementary school principal and teacher. She created Nicky Moonbeam, The Man in the Moon as a child of seven. As a child, Wanda was afraid of the dark. To calm her fears, her father, Edward Clifford Askins, told Wanda and her twin, Fonda that God hung the moon, "as a Night Light in the Sky" for all the "children of the world." After all the children were in bed, The Man in the Moon would stretch his long moonbeam arms around the earth to give each child a hug before they crossed into dreamland whispering, "DON'T BE AFRAID OF THE DARK."

Wanda holds a B.S. degree in History, Political Science, and Sociology from Austin Peay State University. She received scholarships to work on her Master's degree at Kent State University and Middle Tennessee State University with emphasis in Early Childhood Curriculum and Special Education. Wanda was selected as an Outstanding Young Women of America, 1980, and prior in 1976 for her contributions to children, and in 1971, selected as an Outstanding Elementary Teacher of America. Nicky Moonbeam Saves Christmas is the first in the series of, Don't Be Afraid of the Dark! Currently, Wanda is a National Sales Director in the Pharmaceutical and Human Nutrition industry. Wanda and her husband, Chris live in Mission Viejo, CA with their two Greyhounds.

Printed in the United States
By Bookmasters